More Than Meets the Eye
Made in His Image

Unveil your hidden gems and become your true and complete expression

More Than Meets the Eye
Made in His Image

Unveil your hidden gems and become your true and complete expression

By Angelia Hayes

AJH PUBLISHING

Copyright © 2024: Angelia Hayes

ISBN: 9798320076157

Photographer: Ethan Yizong Xie
Powerful Journey Author's Academy, phyllisjenkins.com
Cover Designed by Jackie Castle
First Editor: Lori Vallot-Baskin
Second Editor: Paula Peckham
Formatted: Paula Peckham

Unless otherwise noted, all scripture references in this book are taken from *The Amplified® Bible*, Copyright © 2015 by the Lockman Foundation. Used by permission. (www.Lockman.org) All rights reserved.

Scriptures noted as KJV are quotations taken from the Authorized (King James) Version. Rights in the Authorized Version in the United Kingdom are vested in the Crown. Reproduced by permission of the Crown's patentee, Cambridge University Press.

If noted as NLT, scripture quotations are taken from the *Holy Bible, New Living Translation,* copyright © 1996, 2004, 2007, 2013 by Tyndale House Foundation. Used by permission of Tyndale House Publishers, Inc., Carol Stream, Illinois 60188. All rights reserved.

Scriptures noted as NET are quotations taken from the *New English Translation*. Scripture and/or notes quoted by permission. Quotations designated (NET) are from the NET Bible® copyright © 1996–2006 by Biblical Studies Press, L.L.C All rights reserved.

All rights reserved. No part of this publication may be reproduced, stored in a retrieval system, or transmitted in any form or by any means, electronic or mechanical, including photocopying and recording, without the prior written permission of the author, except for brief quotations in reviews.

NO AI TRAINING: Without in any way limiting the author's (and publisher's) exclusive rights under copyright, any use of this publication to "train" generative artificial intelligence (AI) technologies to generate text is expressly prohibited. The author reserves all rights to license uses of this work for generative AI training and development of machine learning language models.

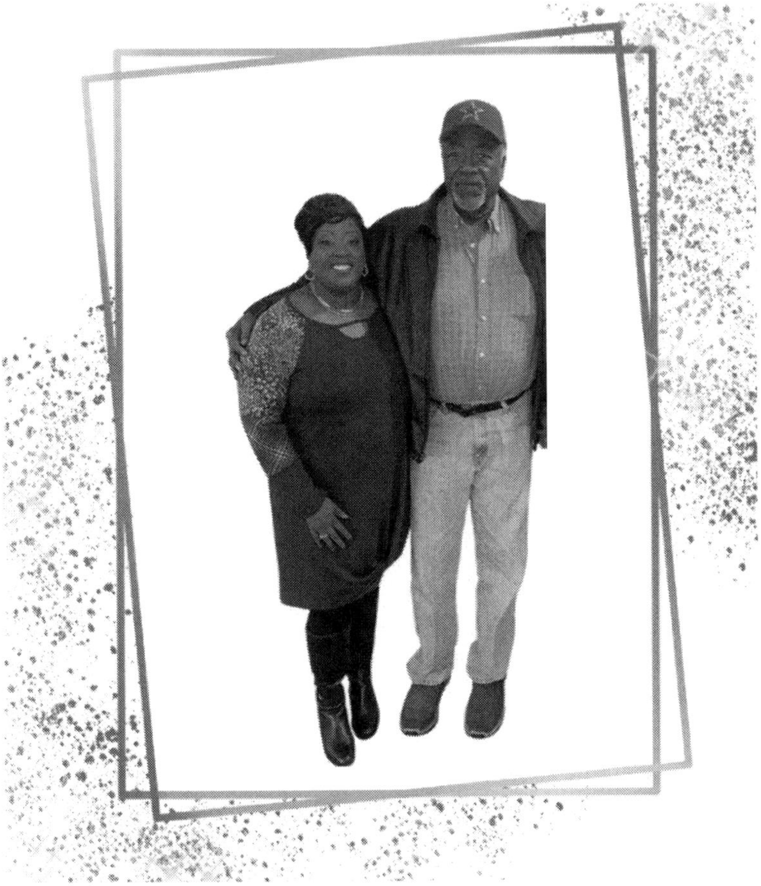

DEDICATION

This book is dedicated to and in honor of my father, Alonzo Smith, a.k.a. Stormy. I am forever grateful for the day we finally met, and I was able to realize you were always the missing piece to my DNA puzzle. Thank you for never denying me as your daughter and holding that special place within your heart for yours truly.

Love you always, Angelia Hayes

TABLE OF CONTENTS

INTRODUCTION 11
Chapter 1 DNA and ME 17
Chapter 2 Dare to Be Different...23
Chapter 3 Changing Your View 27
Chapter 4 Push Past the Past..33
Chapter 5 My Words Matter...41
Chapter 6 Building Tools for Your Inner Self..................47

FOREWARD

I have had the privilege of knowing Angelia, affectionately known to many as "Angie", for over forty years. I was a college student studying at the University of Houston, and Angie and her family attended the same church as I did. Angie, at the time, was a pre-teenager and very quiet and shy. Our pastor at the time was Eddie Pitre-Leadon, and she had a way of putting you out there and exercising your gifts and talents–even if you didn't know you had any. She would have Angie sing in front of the congregation, much to her reluctance.

Angie was so shy; she would sing with her eyes closed the entire time. Her older sister was more extroverted and would gladly play the piano and sing. For many years, Angie was content being Sandra's little sister and staying in her shadow–a safe place where she didn't have to be in the limelight and the center of attention.

As the years passed, I saw Angie open her eyes and see that she could emerge from the shadows and stand boldly in the light of her Lord and Savior, Jesus Christ. She realized God had truly blessed her with gifts and talents that were previously hidden but were now ready to be showcased before the world.

Angie morphed from that shy, quiet caterpillar to the beautiful, elegant butterfly she is today.

She has experienced hurt, and disappointment, betrayal, and rejection, but has learned that God will always work things out for the good.

Angie has learned that everything she experienced in life played a part in shaping her purpose and destiny and helped her become the mighty woman of God she is today.

This book, *More than Meets the Eye*, is a quick read but jammed packed with so many valuable nuggets to help you unpack your hidden potential and discover your true worth in Jesus Christ. The exercises and declarations are designed to help you reflect and realize what a precious jewel you are within the body of Christ. The Master has need of you!

He sees beyond what the natural eye can see and desires for you to bear much fruit for the Kingdom. Get ready to utilize the practical tips in this book, along with the word of God, and be transformed into the woman God has called you to be. Are you ready? Let's go!

Jacqueline L. Higgins, MS, LPC

INTRODUCTION

Beloved, thank you for adding this book to your life's journey. It is with immense joy and love that I'm truly excited to share with you how I began to experience the changes I desired for my life! As you work through this book and the tools provided, I encourage you to BE INTENTIONAL on this purpose journey and exercise patience with yourself. Intentionality combined with patience served as my reminder when I decided to dig in and do the work for self-development.

The three simple practices that have been indicative of active change happening in my life have helped me tremendously, and I believe they will help you as you apply some practical principles and work exercises.

1. Find a quiet space that is special to you and conducive to your growth.

2. Initially, take a few minutes to be still and sit in complete silence. (This is to quieten your mind and calm your spirit.)

3. Remove yourself and disconnect from all distractions (especially your cell phone and other devices).

Here, you are reminded to "Stop your striving and recognize that I am God!" (Psalm 46:10 NET).

Have you ever worked and worked to change yourself? Have you tried to make something happen by controlling the situation? Or perhaps you've wanted to acquire the attention of someone with influence, power, or leadership, or maybe it was a parent, supervisor, teacher. You hoped they would at least recognize your hard work and efforts. Or have a word of encouragement, commendation, and appreciation that would motivate you to keep pressing forward. And this nonsense seems to extend into each area of your life. Well, now is the time to stop, turn, and focus your lenses on the internal dialogue happening from inside yourself.

Now is the time to confront the unpleasant, ugly truths of you; in other words, becoming self-aware of what's brewing from the depths of your soul. There's so much hidden potential and greatness within you, lying dormant, ready to be activated and mobilized for the sake of humanity and our society.

Let me be transparent for a moment here. It was in 2018 that I made a bold decision to terminate a toxic and demeaning relationship with a gentleman who lacked the mental and emotional bandwidth to receive the genuine love I was working to give. Let me say he was incapable of receiving and appreciating the love I was genuinely trying to express.

As the relationship continued, I began to observe his competitive, jealous, and insecure spirit. What do I mean? He seemed more concerned about competing against me than learning how to collaborate as a team. My sister, have you ever experienced this type of man? And how did it make you feel? Were you able to successfully converse with him, especially when you did not see eye to eye? Were you able to reason with each other? Or agree to disagree and eventually come to a mutual understanding?

When I reflected on some of his condescending words and immature behavior, I finally realized he was a young boy encased in a man's body and still had a lot of growing to do.

Doesn't every woman desire a mate with whom she can share her dreams and visions and then willingly support and cheer each other along life's journey? After all, we are on the same team, and the last I checked, to become a winning team, one vital component required is for you to have a mindset of cooperation. However, this brother had another plan; I was obviously not his missing piece.

Have you ever experienced a silent war between you and someone else? It's as if you can sense a quiet tension that manifests each time you and that person are together. Well, it's certainly no walk in the park; however, this underlying, consistent, and unseen struggle always happens between the two. Maybe it's that battle of the sexes! Guess what, beloved, this type of relationship never blossoms because it lacks the capacity for understanding, communication, forgiveness, and growth; it only sinks deeper and deeper into a low place, and as a result, it will suppress some of your most valuable God-given abilities.

As you continue to read, I have provided four key components that shifted me into a new mindset of learning and taking immediate action on the knowledge gained. These are the places in my life that I began to identify and do the work:

- Identity
- Image
- Purpose
- Self-acceptance and self-worth

Sometimes, we can have the theology of a thing enveloped within us, but still, there must come a moment in our lives when we begin to honestly and wholeheartedly confront those blockages, mental blind spots, and demons preventing us from moving forward and becoming the true and complete expression of who God created us to be. In the following Scriptures, there's proof that you were created for productivity, success, and dominance.

"So God created man in his own image, in the image and likeness of God He created him; male and female He created them.

And God blessed them [granting them certain authority] and said to them, "Be fruitful, multiply, and fill the earth, and subjugate it [putting it under your power]; and rule over (dominate) the fish of the sea, the birds of the air, and every living thing that moves upon the earth" (Genesis 1:27-28).

This scripture implies both man and woman were created like the Father, and both were blessed and given the authority to produce and procreate together in the earth's realm. Oh, precious one, you can do all things with the power and strength of our Lord and Savior, Jesus Christ. In my journey, I have learned that before I'm united with my purpose partner, there's some personal development needed on my part.

NOW LET'S GET STARTED!

Arise, my beautiful sister, and give voice to your unique sound of Power!

Do you know the sound you possess resonates in the heart of the earth to transform people's minds and touch the hearts of humanity?

Do you know God created you in such a way that mirrors his image and his likeness?

Do you know the very essence in which God created you offers a sweet fragrance of love permeating every environment?

Do you know natural beauty is within your inner aesthetic makeup? If you have yet to make these remarkable discoveries, begin by speaking to yourself and say, "I am an exceptional gift delivered to this earth fashioned like no one else!"

Chapter 1 DNA and ME

Accepting The Father's Love

Seemingly, it is easier to accept a love you see every day rather than one whom you've never known. Whether you are a daughter or a son, an earthly father's presence reassures your heart's security and gives peace and balance to your insecure emotions. Sometimes through life, we may have a King David experience, asking, "My God, my God, why have you forsaken me?" (Psalm 22:1).

Have you ever been there in anguish, agony, or distress to the point it felt like the Lord has left you alone? All the while, you're praying and praying, and it seems as if nothing is changing. Stop right here! I want to pause and release a word of strength and hope; be encouraged your Father is at work on your behalf. Everything is being arranged and re-arranged in your favor and for your good!

Commit these words to memory. "And we know [with great confidence] that God [who is deeply concerned about us] causes all things to work together [as a plan] for good for those who love God, to those who are called according to His plan and purpose" (Romans 8:28).

As you courageously apply these basic tenets of beliefs to your life, a new person you have yet to encounter will progressively transform and emerge from inside you. *Caution:* there will be days you will feel like waving the white flag in surrender. Sometimes, you will even feel fear, but notice I said *feel* fear. It is guaranteed to present itself; however, you will not succumb to its tactics or intimidation.

REPEAT these words: "For God did not give us a spirit of timidity or cowardice or fear, but [He has given us a spirit] of power and of love and of sound judgment and personal discipline [abilities that result in a calm, well-balanced mind, and self-control]" (2 Timothy 1:7).

I now invite you to take a glimpse into my journey of truth.

Little did I know on November 1, 2022, I would receive a revelation that would be a missing piece to my DNA puzzle. On this afternoon, while working at home, I took a break from the computer. I laid down in the early afternoon for a power nap. After about an hour, I awoke to the ring of my cell phone on the couch beside me. When I came to myself and viewed the number that was calling, I hesitated for a moment. My standard practice is not to answer a phone call when I'm unable to identify the caller, but for some odd reason, this day, I did.

When I answered, a very nice, polite lady immediately greeted me. She stated her name and the community in which she grew up. Okay, and what does that have to do with me? I wondered. Why are you calling?

By this time, I was wide awake, listening attentively to the statements and questions coming from the other end of the call. As the conversation progressed, suddenly, these words hit me.

"You know I'm your sister, right?"

At a complete loss for words, I replied, "No."

She then proceeded to ask, "Do you remember Stormy Smith, who lived on the other side of the bridge? He also had a grass business."

I instantly felt a sting in my forehead. For a moment, complete silence became our conversation. She then asked, "Are you okay?"

I replied, "Yes, I'm fine."

She clearly explained the nature of her call, which was to tell me the truth finally. Perhaps you've experienced a time when a personal reality was revealed to you after many days, months, or, for instance, in my situation, forty-nine years! At this point, I didn't know what to think.

Instantly, I reflected on some childhood scenarios. Mmm, some things seemed to make sense, but then I thought, naw, maybe not. By this time, I was confused and blown away by the abrupt news. However, I concluded our conversation by stating I would definitely need to confirm this information with my mother.

Once the call ended, I sat in disbelief. Suddenly, I started to question God. What was that? Is this true, Lord? What am I going to do? Is this why my skin tone is darker than my siblings? How will this change our relationship? Did my grandparents know before they passed away? Why didn't my mother tell me all these years? And if Mr. Smith is my father, why didn't he say something before now? Whew!

One thing I realized that day is it only takes one phone call, one incident, one experience to change your life. Take a moment and reflect on some of your life experiences.

1. Do you recall a time when you received unexpected and daunting news that perhaps shook you to the core or disturbed your peace?

_____
_____
_____

2. How did you feel in that moment?

_____
_____
_____

3. What were your thoughts?

_____
_____
_____

List your reflections:
1. The Experience/News

_____
_____
_____

2. Feelings

_____
_____
_____

3. Thoughts

_____

_____

_____

Repeat this prayer: Lord, I confess you are the Son of the living God, and I receive your endless love into my heart now. Teach me, Oh Lord, to love like you and embrace all people with your heart.

Congratulations! You have completed your first exercise. This book provides practical tools and exercises for knowledge, growth, and development. Why have I included valuable tools in this book? It is one of my greatest secrets to my success, choosing to commit to personal development, immediately implementing what I learned in daily living, and utilizing the resources and tools at my disposal has been the key that has unlocked my mind and a catalyst to discovering the seeds of potential that were lying dormant within me. Dear sister, I encourage you to do your personal (internal) work! I promise you will never regret the time and effort you decide to invest. As you persist in creating an evolution for your life, the trajectory of your path will lead you on a fantastic journey of discovery.

Chapter 2 Dare to Be Different

"You're a masterpiece. Dare to be different."
~Angelia Hayes

Has there ever been a moment in life when you asked, who am I? Why do I look this way? Why do I sound like this? Why don't I fit into certain groups, circles, and relationships? Of all my friends, why am I singled out to be picked on? Is it the way I dress or style my hair? Or it could be my smooth, deep skin tone, athleticism, academic skill, and unique talents.

As I reflect on my younger days when I attended public schools, I began to notice and hear the harsh criticism of some of my fellow schoolmates during my sixth- through eighth-grade years in junior high. This shy, quiet, reserved, dark-skinned girl slowly internalized the critics' comments, and I questioned my ability to be accepted by others.

On some days, to avoid certain bullies between classes, I would quietly approach my locker, hoping to be practically invisible. At these moments, I would hear comments; "Who does she think she is?" "Oh, she thinks she's cute," or "She thinks she's better than us." "Why doesn't she talk to us?" "I cannot stand her."

Reflecting on those experiences and the negative noise buzzing around me, I discovered that on life's journey, our uniqueness sets us apart. Unfortunately, in many instances, our different qualities agitate the fear and insecurities of individuals who refuse to accept us.

You may be in a place of life where you are asking, "Who am I?" Understanding your genetic background and seed of origin is essential for the journey.

Remember in Chapter One how my missing DNA piece came to light? Let's start from the beginning. As you continue life's journey, the unfolding mysteries will blend like a piece of mosaic art.

The Book of Life submits we are created in God's image and likeness (Genesis 1:27). Just as a manufacturer builds a vehicle, to comprehend your intrinsic mechanism, you must return to the product's designer to gain knowledge of the true essence of your existence. At this point in life, you may not have realized it, or perhaps no one ever said that you are a gem.

Let's define a gem in reference to a person. It is someone valued in a high manner for the quality of their character or beauty. Believe it or not, you fit the description perfectly.

Identity

According to Mirriam-Webster, identity is defined as:

a: the distinguishing character or personality of an individual: individuality;

b: as in personality, the set of qualities that make a person different from other people.

Identity is also your uniqueness, distinctiveness, and peculiarity.

This chapter will explore your personality traits and examine how they integrate into your everyday life in dealing with others. The assessment will help you discover qualities that have continuously lived within you. It will also confirm most of what you have known about yourself but could not articulate to others.

Let's be honest and admit there are days we do not understand ourselves. We currently live in a time where so much emphasis is placed on outward appearances. Everywhere we look, it seems women's bodies are exploited and must be the perfect size, shape, or shade. I must admit, for years, I bought into this ridiculous standard and measurement of what a beautiful woman looks like.

How about you? Do you recall a time in life when you believed the opinion of others more than your own, or better yet, what God has already said about you? Were there voices inside your mind constantly reminding you of your appearance compared to someone else? Word to the wise, precious woman: learn that true beauty resides in your heart. Proverbs 31:30a says it best: "Charm and grace are deceptive, and [superficial] beauty is vain."

Now ask yourself:

What precious jewels do I possess?
_____
_____
_____

At the end of the book, I have provided a free personality assessment for you to take.

I suggest setting aside some time before you embark on the next section and take the assessment. Be sure to read thoroughly, then save your results.

Image

Image is defined at Dictionary.com as:
a. A physical likeness or representation of a person, animal, or thing, photographed, painted, sculptured, or otherwise made visible.
b. To picture or represent in the mind; imagine; conceive.

"You are a God idea."

~Angelia Hayes

Chapter 3 Changing Your View

As women, we naturally grow and develop through life's phases. Sometimes, we may view ourselves in the mirror as beautiful; at other times, we see ourselves as not so attractive. Ladies, we can become our worst critics while we dissect and pick away the things we think are not accepted in society or rejected by others. Have you ever been guilty of these absurd thoughts? Full transparency here—I have entertained that false idea and illusion about myself. So yes, it happens to some of the world's brightest, brilliant, gorgeous, and intelligent ladies.

Exercise: Hey, grab a mirror. Real quick, please take sixty seconds to view yourself in it. Now, make a written note of what you observed by answering the following questions:

1. What about yourself do you recall seeing? (be specific)

_____

_____

2. Were you happy with your reflection?
     Yes ____ No ____

3. If yes, name what you liked.

_____
_____
_____

4. If no, name it.

_____
_____
_____

5. Ask yourself, why was I satisfied or unsatisfied?

_____
_____
_____

As you continue to grow and develop, you will come to realize, it's not important what others think or say about you. What matters is how you view yourself, what you say, and what you think about yourself. Multiple things influence our minds today. For instance, we encounter media from various angles: the arts, entertainment, social sites, movies, books, and music. We hear negative words, conceivably from childhood, relationships, teachers, preachers, employers, and more.

As you live this life, I cannot stress enough how important it is to learn to see yourself from God's perspective. Why, you might ask?

Many opportunities will present themselves for you to compromise your values, confuse your mind, contaminate your soul, and deny your Creator. For example, on my journey, I encountered several guys who were more interested in my body, looks, and how they could benefit rather than being interested in me as a whole person. During these stages of life, I was not rooted and grounded in the Word of God and knowledgeable of what He has predestined for my life.

The truth of the matter is my biological father never affirmed and validated me as a young girl. Most times, the absence of the father's role sends us on a hunt for acceptance and love in all the wrong places. This happens within our subconscious while we are weak, vulnerable, and living in a place of insecurity. Believe it or not, our enemy (Satan) is always seeking a way to devour us and keep us from the blessed plan and purpose God has prearranged for us.

In 1 Peter 5:8-9, it reads, "Be sober [well balanced and self-disciplined], be alert and cautious at all times. That enemy of yours, the devil, prowls around like a roaring lion [fiercely hungry], seeking someone to devour. But resist him, be firm in your faith [against his attack—rooted, established, immovable], knowing that the same experiences of suffering are being experienced by your brothers and sisters throughout the world. [You do not suffer alone.]"

Indeed, I've not always dotted every "i" or crossed every "t." Frequently, I've fallen, slipped, tripped, and dipped in and out of various temptations, but God's eternal love, abundant grace, and everlasting mercies rescued me from self-destruction!

Let's not forget his divine protection. In my early teens, my mother shared with me a very profound insight. She said one day, while I was young, I played. God showed her three angels surrounding me. It was then she knew God had assigned an angelic shield around me to protect and guard me throughout my lifespan. My prayer is this: The LORD bless you, and keep you [protect you, sustain you, and guard you]; The LORD make His face shine upon you [with favor], And be gracious to you [surrounding you with lovingkindness]; The LORD lift up His countenance (face) upon you [with divine approval], And give you peace [a tranquil heart and life] (Numbers 6:24-26).

Woman, arise, lift your head, and say loud and clear, "I am more than what the natural eyes can see!"

At times on my journey, I could see all the beautiful things about someone else, but didn't see the worth and value within me. As my walk with God continued, and His Word came alive within me, I discovered how special I am, and all the many valuable treasures buried inside.

A foundational scripture from which I continue to build and grow in faith and confidence states: We now have this light shining in our hearts, but we ourselves are like fragile clay jars containing this great treasure. This makes it clear that our great power is from God, not from ourselves (2 Corinthians 4:7 NLT).

Think about that for a minute: we were born into the world loaded with priceless goods.

At the time of conception, you were planted as a seed in the womb of your mother (the carrier or incubator). From our seed state, we formed and grew into an identifiable image of a baby. As you were nurtured and fed, you encountered three trimesters of growth. All these stages were necessary for your growth and development in preparation for the great delivery! You may start small, but God has a remarkable future ahead. For you to live from a place of authenticity and freedom, the prerequisite is to do the work of self-mastery. Remember, once you landed on the scene of life, you arrived loaded with a wealth of talents and gifts waiting to be discovered. So, sis, you owe it to yourself and, oh! not to mention, people around you and those you have yet to meet who will benefit.

Now, take some time to work through this next exercise in a quiet place. Keep a running list to continuously build upon.

Exercise: Create a list of your gifts, talents, skills, and abilities.

Chapter 4 Push Past the Past

For it is [not your strength, but it is] God who is effectively at work in you, both to will and to work [that is, strengthening, energizing, and creating in you the longing and the ability to fulfill your purpose] for His good pleasure (Philippians 2:13).

Let's take a moment to reflect on the scripture above. Immanuel, God with us, is always here to support us. Isaiah 7:14.

While He faithfully and consistently performs in his role, we are not without responsibility to accomplish those things we've been called to do. Here are some key factors for you to inscribe into your mind while on this journey of self-mastery and development.

1. Be a person of decision. Make up your mind!

2. Let determination be your driving force. Be diligent!

3. Be willing to cultivate your soil. Do the work!

4. Embrace the process while understanding it's a lifetime journey. Commit to yourself!

Have you ever been accused of being stubborn, inflexible, strong-willed, or purposeful? If you relate or identify with any of those traits, it simply means you have the power to decide. The power to decide what? Your anticipated future.

God has graciously granted us everything we need to carry out our purpose. He has also custom-fitted us for our unique assignments. The passage in Genesis reads, "And I will make of thee a great nation, and I will bless thee, and make thy name great; and thou shall be a blessing:" (Genesis 12:2 KJV). So the valuables within your treasure box were not planted there for you only, but were delivered to you as a gift to enrich people you love and will encounter on life's journey.

My friend, please do us all a favor and invest the time in developing yourself. Do this so that humanity may experience the whole essence of who you are predestined to become. Do not despise these small beginnings. To reach your potential, I encourage you to embrace and endure the cultivation process. The personal return on your investments (ROI) will yield dividends beyond your wildest imagination!

Purpose

The Oxford English dictionary defines purpose as:

The reason for which something is done or made or for which it exists.

It also means cause, reason, plan, goal, value, worth, and intention.

Has anyone ever said you are an accident or mistake? Well, I have good news: despite the complex circumstances or series of events around how you were conceived, God planned for you to be here!

When I graduated from high school in 1991, I looked forward to attending college at Lamar University. My sister was a year older than me, so she preceded me in going off to school. I had passed my SAT, received my acceptance letter, and was approved for all my financial assistance. All prerequisites were satisfied, and I was on track to enter the college environment in the fall of 1991. With great anticipation and excitement, I joined my sister and started my first semester away from home at Lamar University.

Thank goodness, because I became known as "Sandra's sister"; everyone received me with love and open arms. In all honesty, I began this new path with a bit of fear and anxiety, but I was determined to learn and achieve my intended purpose of earning my college degree.

Have you ever had a great desire to accomplish a specific goal? Something you worked toward?

Gradually, I lost the passion and desire for what I originally planned. My mind became cluttered with confused thoughts. The weight and pressure from familiar voices and external forces played on my emotions, and I was tempted to participate in illicit activities. Then I disconnected and withdrew from the intended assignment and resources afforded to me.

For me, it was my classes, friends, and instructors. As I took matters into my own hands and lived out my freedom rights of being away from home, my college track shifted in another direction.

Have you ever found yourself leaving a set pathway designed for your success?

In the spring semester of my second year at Lamar University, one of my roommates introduced me to a young man. He was friends with the guy she was currently dating. I should have known something wasn't quite right when I learned he had just become a young father with his supposed ex-girlfriend.

Because of my fast connection with him, my focus quickly became blurry, and my attention diverted. I began missing class assignments, and because my grades dropped, I withdrew from a class. It's with sincerity I share with you how easily derailment can happen.

Let's view it from the perspective of a train. When a derailment occurs, it's an accident in which a train comes off its track. Why? There are several reasons.

1. A collision with another object.
2. A conductor error.
3. Mechanical track failure.
4. Broken rails or defective wheels.

Needless to say, there was nothing wrong with the track I was initially guided to by the support of my mother, family, and educators. Nor was there a problem with the tools or resources established.

Still, unbeknown to me at the time, there was brokenness, dissatisfaction and many personal defects residing within my soul. These unconsciously caused me to make moves and decisions I later regretted.

See, this young man's motives concerning me were not pure or positive. His only purpose was to have a good time and score another point (if you know what I mean).

As a result of our short-lived physical relationship, I became pregnant. Immediately after my last physical encounter with him, it was like I instantly knew from deep within that a seed was planted. Once I confirmed what I knew to be true, I ultimately decided to go through with an abortion. Was I happy with my decision? Not at all. I remember being at the lowest point of my life: secluded, withdrawn, sad, and depressed, with feelings of regret, shame, and unforgiveness. Having fallen into a deep, dark pit, I had suicidal thoughts and extremely negative internal dialogue. I was brought up and reared to have moral values in an environment filled with love. The words "God will never forgive me for this awful decision" repeatedly played in my mind like a broken record. The world around me was dark, and I thought there was no reason for me to live. What was the purpose? God is mad at me, and my loved ones must think I'm the worst person in the world. From my heart to yours, stay on the assigned track.

Exercise: Take a few minutes to reflect and record.
- Have you experienced a personal collision with someone?

    Yes ____ No ____
- Who, When, Where?

_____
_____
_____

- Identify some of your most crucial errors and/or mistakes.

_____

_____

_____

- Now repent and forgive yourself for any damages caused by your experiences.

_____

_____

_____

Pray this prayer (aloud).

Have mercy on me, O God,
   because of your unfailing love.
Because of your great compassion,
   blot out the stain of my sins.
Wash me clean from my guilt.
   Purify me from my sin.
For I recognize my rebellion;
   it haunts me day and night.
Against you, and you alone, have I sinned;
   I have done what is evil in your sight.
You will be proved right in what you say,
   and your judgment against me is just.
For I was born a sinner—
   yes, from the moment my mother conceived me.
But you desire honesty from the womb,
   teaching me wisdom even there.
Purify me from my sins, and I will be clean;
   wash me, and I will be whiter than snow.
Oh, give me back my joy again;

you have broken me—
now let me rejoice.
Don't keep looking at my sins.
Remove the stain of my guilt.
Create in me a clean heart, O God.
Renew a loyal spirit within me.
Do not banish me from your presence,
and don't take your Holy Spirit from me.
Restore to me the joy of your salvation,
and make me willing to obey you.
Then I will teach your ways to rebels,
and they will return to you.
Forgive me for shedding blood, O God who saves;
then I will joyfully sing of your forgiveness.
Unseal my lips, O Lord,
that my mouth may praise you.
You do not desire a sacrifice, or I would offer one.
You do not want a burnt offering.
The sacrifice you desire is a broken spirit.
You will not reject a broken and repentant heart, O God.
Look with favor on Zion and help her;
rebuild the walls of Jerusalem.
Then you will be pleased with sacrifices offered in the right spirit—
with burnt offerings and whole burnt offerings.
Then bulls will again be sacrificed on your altar
(Psalm 51: 1-19 NLT).

Chapter 5 My Words Matter

Death and life are in the power of the tongue, And those who love it and indulge it will eat its fruit and bear the consequences of their words (Proverbs 18:21).

Often in life, things happen or simply appear, so we think, in the form of a blessing, problem, challenge, or a complex situation. Somewhere along the journey, we have been led to believe it just happened, and now the frequent use of the famous statement "it is what it is" has led some to think that's the way it should be, and things will never change.

Often, we conform and accept things at face value, thinking we have no control at all. Listen up. We all contain the power to frame our world by the words that proceed out of our mouths! Therefore, the words you speak today will manifest in your future by establishing the course of your life. So, if you want to know what your life will look like in ten, five, or even one year, listen to the words coming out of your mouth.

Although someone has convinced you what others say and think of you matters, the actual truth is that it's what you say about yourself that makes the difference! For instance:

"I'll never get out of debt."

"I'll never get well."

"I'll never recover from this setback."

"I'll never get over this bad breakup."

"I'll never break this addiction."

"I'll never marry the love of my life."

"I will never forgive them."

When you release words into the atmosphere, they begin to shape and form your reality. You can't speak poverty and have prosperity. You can't speak defeat and have victory. You can't speak sickness and have good health. You can't speak hate and experience true love.

PERSONAL ANNOUNCEMENT: Pay close attention to what you say about yourself, your family, your finances, your health, your business, and every aspect of your life! Beloved, it is important that you start now establishing a healthy habit of speaking words of victory, blessing, abundance, and favor over your life and into the lives of those you love.

So now you are aware you have in your possession the ability to set, shift, and change the direction of your life? When you utilize the tools provided in this book, people, places, and things will take on a new meaning. Your life will transform, and deep from within, a newness of life will spring forth. Our Lord reminded his enemy of this power by simply responding, "It is written and forever remains written; MAN (referring to us, humanity) SHALL NOT LIVE BY BREAD ALONE, BUT BY EVERY WORD THAT COMES OUT OF THE MOUTH OF GOD" (Matthew 4:4).

I would be remiss if I didn't caution you of some enemies you might encounter along the way. To name a few, your enemies can wear the face of fear, uncertainty, negativity, frustration, procrastination, doubt, insecurity, discrimination, rejection, abandonment, and abuse. To conquer and overcome these hurdles, one must first identify one's enemies; give them an exit from one's mind, body, and soul; and then replace the ill-spoken words with words that spring forth new life! What you do here cancels out the evil report of your enemy and creates a new story for your future.

Understand your voiceprint is amazingly unique! Commence to using it to shift your own life in the direction of God's promised plan. For it's not what others say Jeremiah reminds us of the blessed plan. "For I know the plans and thoughts that I have for you, says the LORD, plans for peace and well-being and not for disaster, to give you a future and a hope" (Jeremiah 29:11)

These words were spoken to God's chosen people while they were exiled from their native country in captivity at the hands of their enemy. You may have been rejected, abandoned, or feel isolated even now, but you can be emancipated, healed, and restored to your destined place of joy, love, victory, and prosperity! Now let's quit allowing the noise from other people to dictate your future and let's become proactive by speaking, creating, and transforming our future!

Words of Empowerment

Our Father God is a multi-faceted diamond in his creation of humankind. He's an incredible artist who paints every picture with strokes of beauty and grace, a mastermind of diversity while developing every piece into a well-crafted artistry. As a skilled potter, His hands have formed, shaped, and molded every detail to his satisfaction, calling it good! Isaiah reminds us, Yet, O LORD, You are our Father; We are the clay, and You are the Potter, And we all are the work of Your hand (Isaiah 64:8).

Beloved, your life has tremendous meaning and significance! You must never forget how fearfully and wonderfully you are designed. God created you in a complex manner, so much so there's not one replica of you in this world, nor will there ever be in the future.

As you continue to evolve and witness your organic growth from the inside out, I have provided ten declarations below for you to speak and declare daily over yourself.

DAILY DECLARATIONS

1. I AM a child of God fully accepted by the Father.
2. I AM loved by God, regardless of how I perform.
3. I AM forgiven, and I will not be tormented by my past errors and mistakes.
4. I AM a new creature pre-destined for greatness.
5. I AM an overcomer, and my faith is changing my circumstances.
6. I AM the expression of God in the earth, unlimited and unmatched.

7. I AM an overcomer.
8. I AM enough and have everything I need to succeed.
9. I AM healed, whole, and free to live the life God has purposed for me.
10. God is on my side, and I will not fear.

Chapter 6 Building Tools for Your Inner Self

But you, beloved, build yourselves up on [the foundation of] your most holy faith [continually progress, rise like an edifice higher and higher], pray in the Holy Spirit, and keep yourselves in the love of God (Jude 1:20-21).

Therefore, if you have been raised with Christ, keep seeking the things above, where Christ is, seated at the right hand of God. Keep thinking about things above, not things on the earth, for you have died, and your life is hidden with Christ in God (Colossians 3:1-3 NET).

No need to worry about your life's journey of purpose; we are encapsulated (enclosed and wrapped up in the Father's care). While you continue to walk and rest in his unfailing love, the pieces will all come together as a beautiful work of art.

So stand firm and hold your ground, HAVING TIGHTENED THE WIDE BAND OF TRUTH (personal integrity, moral courage) AROUND YOUR WAIST AND HAVING PUT ON THE BREASTPLATE OF RIGHTEOUSNESS (an upright heart) (Ephesians 6.14).

For we are his workmanship, created in Christ Jesus for good works, which God hath before ordained that we should walk in them (Ephesians 2:10 KJV).

In Him also we have received an inheritance [a destiny—we were claimed by God as His own], having been predestined (chosen, appointed beforehand) according to the purpose of Him who works everything in agreement with the counsel and design of His will (Ephesians 1:11).

God saw everything that He had made, and behold, it was very good, and He validated it completely (Genesis 1:31).

"You have been marked (stamped, sealed) for GREATNESS!"

~Angelia Hayes

Quotes for Growth

"Open your treasure box; priceless valuables are locked up inside of you!"

"Your inside will display your true life; LOL (Live out Loud)

"Know your worth; You are a unique design crafted by God."

"Your life is your story. Write well. Edit often and create your narrative."

~Angelia Hayes

In conclusion, it has been a blessed honor to impart and share some of my valley experiences, times of vulnerability, and moments in life when I was lost, confused, hurt, hopeless, and without the everlasting love of Jesus. Once I first confessed with my mouth and began to believe in my heart the Lord himself sacrificed his entire life just for me, all the wrong, self-defeating thoughts, self-sabotaging decisions, and violations I had committed were forgiven and washed in the blood of Jesus from my past, present, and future.

As I continued on my journey with him and building my relationship, it was eventually revealed to me that I am *the apple of my father's eye!* (Zechariah 2:8 NET).

Beloved, always keep at the forefront of your mind that you are and forever will be that apple in his eyes, meaning the very pupil. When we think about our natural eye, the pupil is one of the most vulnerable yet valuable parts of our bodies. In consideration of being his pupil, your value and worth are at an all-time high; simply saying, you are a most precious possession valued at an incomputable price. My friends, my sisters, do you realize what this means? Your value is beyond human calculation and measure, unable to be quantified by people, suppressed by difficulties, and prevented by challenges.

"You are destined for greatness and guaranteed to win."

~Angelia Hayes

Special note to singles:
I write to you as one who is presently single but eagerly in hopes and anticipation of connecting with my purpose partner at the appointed time. During this time in your life, I strongly recommend developing a strategy of

intentional focus for personal growth and self-development. You will discover things and identify the people who are wasting your time.

To assist you in this practice, apply and pray the principle from Psalm 90:12: "So teach us to number our days, that we may cultivate and bring to You a heart of wisdom." God's plan and the purpose for which He has called you will unfold as you trust His process and relinquish your will to control each aspect of the journey. At the appropriate time, He will gently merge that right person on the path of your journey, and then you will fully understand the extent of the wait.

Encouragement to single women and moms:
The Word of God is the secret sauce to your success and anything you pursue and are blessed to accomplish. If you are a single mom, my prayer is that God will grant you the wisdom, grace, and strength to nurture, teach, and guide your children along life's pathway. Be at peace and do not worry about the love you currently do not possess, but use this season of your life to pray, seek, and ask God for His perfect will to be done in your current situation.

I am here to walk alongside you on this life journey while assisting you in discovering and building your self-image, identity, self-worth, and the unique purpose the Creator has so graciously chosen you to execute while living on the earth. Remember, the Father's love for you transcends all human comprehension, opinions, and criticism, and he will never abandon you, for you are His tailor-made, custom-designed, most valuable jewel.

Now take your assessment in a quiet space.

Exercise: Access your FREE ASSESSMENT @ https://www.16personalities.com/

Notes

Chapter 2

1.	Merriam-Webster "identity"
https://www.merriam-webster.com/dictionary/identity
2.	Dictionary.com "image"
https://www.dictionary.com/browse/image

Chapter 4

1.	Oxford English dictionary "purpose"
https://languages.oup.com/google-dictionary-en/

Chapter 5

1. Free assessment - NERIS Analytics Limited
Nine Hills Road, Cambridge, CB2 1GE, United Kingdom | Registered in England and Wales, # 8646330
www.16personalities.com

WHAT DID YOU LEARN FROM READING *MORE THAN MEETS THE EYE?*

What changes will you make in your life?

SPECIAL ACKNOWLEDGEMENTS

I want to express my deepest gratitude to my mother and sister for all their unwavering love, support and encouragement through my life, even when my path of direction did not seem clear. Thank you for always being there in support of my dreams and for giving me the strength and courage to know I could accomplish my heart's desires.

With much love and gratitude, your daughter and sister, Angelia Hayes.

Write a review on Amazon.com
Connect with Angelia Hayes via Email:
uniquelyyours28@yahoo.com
Website: www.angeliahayestxnotary.com

Like, Follow, Subscribe

Watch **Angelia Hayes** on her YouTube Channel

Unique Foundations Enterprise, LLC
Facebook business page

Thanks for your support!
God Bless!

Be Our Guest on The Angelia Hayes Podcast

"Life With No Limits"

Reach out today to schedule your spot and
let your voice be heard!
Contact ANGELIA at uniquelyyours28@yahoo.com
for booking and inquiries.
Donations can be made to:
Zelle 979-334 2648 or Cash app $angeliahayes
Proceeds will be sent to Life Revision Center, Inc. 501(3c).

More Than Meets the Eye

Made in the USA
Columbia, SC
11 October 2024